Hold My Hand

TALES OF WALKING WITH MY EMOTIONS

Maureen Tierney

BookLeaf
Publishing

India | USA | UK

Presentation by *BookLeaf Publishing*

Web: www.bookleafpub.com

E-mail: info@bookleafpub.com

ISBN: 9789358366228

First edition 2021

"To the Goddesses who feel lost and alone. Know your strength, and know you have never been truly alone."

Acknowledgements

First and foremost, to Natalia. Without you, this book wouldn't have turned out the way it had. From gentle coaching to listening to my turmoil emotions, your constant assistance helped this collection of poems come into being.

To Brittany, for loving my words, encouraging me to keep writing, and your unending enthusiasm and support.

To Danielle, for doing a photography shoot so I could have my first ever real life author photo.

And to BookLeaf Publishing, who if they hadn't run this challenge, I never would have gotten the courage to publish anything.

Preface

The ideas for these poems came from a really low period in my life. I was sitting with such heaviness one day, it felt impossible to return to my shift at work. My friend encouraged me to sit with my emotion. Thus, I met and sat with Sadness.

For each emotion, I would sit, close my eyes, and allow myself to feel what was going on. From there, I had an outline I could use for the poem, when I eventually got to it.

Once I began writing, each Goddess Emotion had a different cadence, different song to her poem's style. I loved seeing how they each turned out, greater and more than I ever could have imagined.

I'm not yet done with these emotions, either. I hope to be able to paint them in watercolor and display them in my room. I know they will never leave me. They will shift and change, as my relationships with them change, but I know they will always be with me.

I hope reading through my journey, my heart, of each of these emotions, gives you a sense of shared feeling, but also the ability to trust yourself, and to sit with your own emotions and feelings. Explore what they look like. And, hopefully, find healing along the way.

1. JOURNEY

Begins with a step

  Just one

Mine has been no different

Months of

  Ups

    Downs

  Ups

    Downs

  Ups

    Downs

Repeating, repeating

  As my poor head spins

I invite you

  to come on my journey with me

    to meet my experiences

My emotions

in all their raw glory

From Sadness

To Hope,

From Disappointment

To Trust,

I invite you

To see these women

Listen to their stories

With the small hope

that they may help you

along your own wild journey.

2. MEETING SADNESS

Overwhelmed

  I sit on my lunch

    But I am far from my food

I close my eyes

  let feeling sweep over me

Sadness

  a sadness so strong

    my breath leaves my body

I open my eyes

  blues of every hue

    sad

    stormy

      greet me

I see her

  Know her in an instant

  Sadness

She sits before

  a pool of tears

    I settle by her side

      Her eyes

        they are endless

          endless pools of tears

Sadness is bent

  her body weighed

    by all that she carries

I expect a voice

  but Sadness utters no word

Lodged in her throat

  stopped by her endless tears

        her mourning

        her loss

I search her face

  Why am I here?

  but I know

I found Sadness

because Sadness weighs upon my soul
I sit by her side
  together
    We cry
      and it begins to rain
I reach to touch her
  my hand comes away wet
    she is only water
      I cannot touch
Minutes
  hours
    days
And my tears ebb
    Sadness still cries
      I think she always will
The water woman Goddess Emotion
    she smiles at me
      lined with sadness
    she smiles

and cups my cheek
Her water lips
  do not move at all
    but a voice speaks in my head
You, darling
  shall be back
    and you shall know more
      of your own soul,
        when you return to me
I am safe

I want to laugh
  but despite the tears
            the water
              the ache
                the weight
                    I believe

Tears prick my eyes
  But Sadness shakes her head

catches the tear

and I feel light as air

though. She looks heavier.

I am your companion

to take your sadness today

Fear not,

she says with a smile

I can hold the weight

where you cannot

I open my mouth

but instead

I close it

nod

Sadness nods, too

You will be back

I promise you that

but with more strength

in your warrior's heart

I take a breath

  and suddenly

    I am in reality

I've returned

  my lunch before me

But I feel her

    Sadness

She sits upon my shoulder

  My guide for the day

3. TRIPLE BODIED GODDESS EMOTION

My chest feels weighted

  Not sure I can breathe

    I close my eyes…

I open them

  returned to Sadness' pool

    though she is not to be seen

I take a shuddering breath

  Not sure who I will meet

    But having a good sense…

It grows dark

  shadows dance

    darker than darkness

Dark as pitch
    but deeper still
        more like a void

Feeling twists
    inside my gut
        but still I walk

I shiver
    not from cold
        I fear who awaits me

The shadow clears
    never shadow at all
        She steps close

Hair so long
    a tangled mess
        reaching to the floor

Nearer, nearer

    till she brushes my cheek

        and I recoil

Another

    hair to her shoulders

        Knotted and wild

Closer still she comes

    brushing my other cheek

        and I shudder once more

A third comes

    hair short, short, short

        the leader of the three

I am overwhelmed

    I think I scream

though I can't be sure

Fright pulses through me
   I quake where I stand
      gripped with three emotions

As I breathe anew
   the ache eases
      and three figures begin to glow

I see them clearer,
   swallow,
      despite my dry throat.

They all reach
   to touch me
      and I don't recoil

Shortest hair,

the leader,

    Scared, speaks

We mean to

  protect you

    she softly says

Longest, tangled hair

  Goddess Emotion Worry

    brushes a tear from my cheek

Scared speaks

  it has gotten out of hand

    we know, sweet child

Fear, the last, nods

  squeezes my shoulder

  You needn't fear us

I want to laugh

  but it catches

    I know she speaks truth

Closer they come

  a triangle formed

    me, their charge, in center

They hold me

  and suddenly

    all I can do is see

Their attempts at safety

  even if Worry is out of hand

    even if Fear creates false scenarios

I take a breath

  tell Worry

    I will tame her tangles

She smiles
  it will shift
    with time

I wonder
  how it was
    she appeared before

But Worry shakes her head
  I do not need that answer
    I need others

Not of the past,
  nor of the future
    But answers for my present

I nod
  deep breath

try to hold them

Harder to hold than Sadness,
  yet still I do
    Worry closest, hair ever growing

It hurts
  to be so worried
    so vulnerable

Scared kisses
  my brow
    offers a reminder

Despite the deep ache
  I am able to be soft
    even as I show a fake thick skin

I whimper

but nod, too

    Her words are true

Worry hugs me

    then quiet Fear

        then wise Scared

Nestled among them

    a promise

        to protect me

Protect

    to let me ache

        be vulnerable

What a luxury

    to only feel

        feel worry, scared, fear

I need not fight

  fake bravery

    build a façade

I can just feel

  they hold me close

    my stomach stills

No longer strangers,

  they hold me close,

    then fade like shadows

4. TWO HALVES OF A BLEEDING WHOLE

A new emotion bubbles inside,

I begin from where I left

Worry, Fear, Scared

following the tug

I know where I'm going

and I am happy to meet her

I find her

sitting in a patch of sun

I smile

I love sunlight

I walk closer

with bold, quick step

nothing Love has could scare me

I come to Love's right

my breath leaving me

Such beauty

I have never seen

absolutely gorgeous

stunning, kind

For a moment,

I am stunned at how much I love her

but then I laugh

I *love* Love

I feel silly,

but it feels good, too

I see Love smile

You heard my call

I nod

I wouldn't have ignored her

What have you to show me?

Come closer

I do,

coming close

stepping fully in front of her

My shriek

barely contained

turned to strangled gasp

this isn't how love should be.

Love sits

half in sunlight, yes

half... half unimaginable

but Love stares

daring me to take her in

      my lesson

      I ache

            but listen

The right

full of beauty

            life

            love

The left

I gasp again

feeling her pain

A barren landscape

full of burns

her eyelid droops

no eye in socket

skin crumbles

flakes with movement

Only a hint of hair

singed to the root

not an ounce of love

to be seen

I stand confused

trying to hide my disgust

but my stomach roils

Why

Love smiles

a half smile

her left a grimace

revealing cracked teeth

You tell me why

I shake my head

I don't know

I don't know

I don't want to know

I don't want to voice the truth

pounding in my heart

Does Love's heart

even beat?

It... *fuck*

it's on the burnt side of her body

Love looks at me

her one eye

boring to my soul

You do know

Tell me

Why, child, have you done this?

I shake my head

I haven't done a thing

I haven't.

Love smiles

You deny to answer

but even that is an answer

Love holds out her left hand

You have neglected

the most important part of love

Only the left side of her lips move

She frightens me

this love I see

I haven't

I try to protest

A lie on my tongue

Love smiles sadly

looks at her right arm

You have

This arm

has never looked better

I am filled with love

the love you have for others

I must be crying

I feel wetness on my cheeks

Love lifts her left arm

But this

You've neglected

a love so important

You've forgotten,

little goddess,

how to love yourself

I gasp in pain

sobbing hard

I don't know how

Love smiles

You do

Love yourself

as you love others

It is possible

Love hands me an image

I see Love

a striking, whole Goddess

She isn't blackened

on one side

Her colors dim

but still

she looks whole

A day I loved myself

You do remember

You do it sometimes

I ache

I don't know how to fix you

Love smiles,

soft and kind

You do

Love yourself

It's the biggest part of love

You

Deserve

Love

The love you give

Please,

give to yourself

I can't

my voice breaks

I can't

Love's smile

turns softer

No

Not yet

But

you will

Until then,

this way

I shall remain

I sob,

aching to do

as Love asks

Love lets me cry

her good hand on my back

I'm so thankful

I cry

lost in the terror

of trying to love

myself

an impossible task

I open my eyes

when my tears dry

I still feel Love

though I'm home again

A new task before me

finding love

for myself

again

5. PLIGHT OF A TITAN

Ache

Ache

Ache

It fills my bones

   I awake to wander

      Knowing who it is

      that I shall find

She's been following

   for days on end

      yet today is the first

      I've found her

I see her

   sitting in a puddle

I walk towards her

   rain begins

Each step

water splashes

Each step

a pain pulls

through my spine

Hunched,

in pain,

it is all my strength

to sit beside her

Ache

Ache

Ache

She is gaunt

I'm full of pain

it is hard to think

Her breathing

jagged

uneven

I match her breath

Or...

 Does she match mine?

Ache

Ache

Ache

She tilts her head

 up to the sky

   screams

   screams

   screams

Her heart

 visible in her chest

   crack

   crack

   cracking

Cracking as she screams

 until it shatters in her chest

Only to rebuild

rebuild

to shatter once more

on her next painful scream

Not a Goddess,

no,

but a punished Titan

aching for relief

And,

I know why she is gaunt

Neck strained

with her forceful cries

Sobs wracking her body

so nothing will stay down

The puddle we sit in

her tears

as much as the rain

her battered body

Ache

Ache

Ache

Her battered body

my battered soul

Ache

Ache

Ache

I ache to sit with her

It hurts

aches

aches

aches

Fuck, it hurts

She shakes as she cries

we add to the pool

Her ribs almost cave

it feels like mine follow

We sit close

  share tears

   and pain

But I feel miles apart from her

We sit beside

  yet I don't know

   how to touch her

So

  we cry

   so close

    our elbows touch

     so far apart

      in our endless pain

Eventually,

  her tears ease

   I'm stunned from mine

    thinking it was never-ending

Ache speaks

No one has ever done that

Just sat

in their pain

as I traverse mine

She cups my cheek

Her hand so warm

Ache speaks

But then,

our pain

it is the same

isn't it?

Learn

to sit in the ache

ache

ache

Wave

after

wave

washing over you

I am not permanent
    but I am important
I am impossible to ignore

To ache is to live

I am not here always
    but when I come,
        feel me
Let me course through your blood
    find clarity when I leave
I can only nod
    ache

    ache

    ache

To ache is to live

It is hard to sit

with ache in my chest

  my body shakes

    it hurts to feel an avalanche

           ache

           ache

           ache

I look up to the sky

  I scream

    scream

    scream

Goddess after all

  I see her story clearer

To ache is to live

  I mustn't hide my pain

To ache is to live

6. SILENT SHIFTER OF THE NIGHT

I wander on

  through the labyrinth

When I come to her,

  I am stunned

    no human stands before me

A large black dog

  joy spikes through me

    before guilt washes over me

I knew I'd see her soon

  but that she is a canine

    it slices to my soul

      I'm leaving my sweet girl

        behind once more

Once the canine

  reaches me,

  she shifts

Terror spikes

   shifting is new

      then Guilt settles

         a blanket of fresh snow

Simple,

   yet she scares me

      a floor length gown

         in ruby red

         and bare feet

Guilt folds her arms

   stares into my soul

      is there an opposite

         of puppy dog eyes?

Guilt stares

   and stares

      and stares

         her eyes an unrelenting color

         I can't pin down

Guilt stares

stares until I fall

  to my knees

    I'm abandoning her

      a blow to my

        already cracked heart

Another

  I'm a burden

    a strike

      impossible not to flinch

Guilt stands tall

  never moving a muscle

I expect things

  I don't deserve

    I don't belong

      and shouldn't bother

With nary a word

  Guilt makes me admit

    each guilt I feel

      with her unending stare

Guilt

  for having family

    and shunning them

Guilt

  for taking up space

Guilt

  for breathing

I bite my lip

  trying to stop

    but that stare...

      Guilt won't let me stop

I bite

  lip

    cheek

      tongue

        tasting blood

Guilt wins

  She doesn't smirk

    but she knew I would crumble

I feel guilty

  for being alive

    I finally whisper

      collapsing to the ground

I can't win

  I don't deserve anything

    I deserve my pain

I deserve this

  I deserve this

  I deserve this

Guilt nods once

  She turns to leave

    Hell Goddess, Silent as Night

She leaves me

  to find the lesson alone

And it takes me

  forever

    broken on the floor

Guilt was

silent

   she didn't speak a word

  she lifted no hand

  she didn't touch

   wasn't near

Guilt is unlike the others

  she doesn't need to lift a finger

   doesn't need to make a sound

I do it all to myself

  Guilt *never* hurt me

I did it all myself

  I hurt myself

   with unimaginable guilt

Guild needn't fight

  I do it all for her

My lesson

  is to change

   shed the guilt

I deserve to be here

I deserve life

I deserve good things

I deserve the world

The lesson is

  the only one

    hurting me

      is myself

But

  there is so much more

Yes

  Guilt may win

    some days

But others

  I win

The lesson is

  finding balance

    and surviving

      managing

        the worst guilty days

Guilt won one day

but I refuse

to let her have them all

7. SAFETY IN THE UNIVERSE'S PURPLE CLOAK

I remain

  where Guilt left me

    oh, so very small

      unable to move

Numb

  on silent, soft limb

comes to me

Numb

  close for weeks

knows I need to face her

Numb

  wise, gentle Goddess

finally has her chance

Numb

  sits on the ground

scoops my small frame close

Numb

  envelops me fully

her deep purple cloak

  a blanket around my soul

Numb

  holds me

    smoothing my hair

Her voice is soft

  soft yet wise

    the weight of the world

      in each word she speaks

I

  know

    this

      is

        not

          what

          you

wish

Her voice

  like the universe

   ancient

   powerful

    a star

   super nova

    black hole

I curl into her

  she soothes my back

I

  know

   it

    is

     not

      ideal

       to

        be

         this

                   way

Time

   she grants me

      between each sentence

Feeling the

           g

           r

           a

           v

           i

           t

           y

   of her words

Let

   me

      take

      you

She takes my pain

   not soothing

it can't go away

she pushes it

wraps me in numbness

in her purple cloak

This

isn't

ideal

We

know

you

aren't

safe

Her whisper

still like

the universe

For

now

let

me

take

you

I nod, softly
It

is

all

I

can

do

And numbness fills me

She is right

A constant

for weeks

months

I would always

always

fight her off

But

But

Being in her purple cloak

  her universe arms

it keeps me

  from disintegrating

My home

  would blow

    my ashes away

      rather than

        piecing me together

Numb promises

  this is not forever

I nod

  I believe her

Numb holds me

  holds me close

The universe will not let me go

The universe will not let me go

When my mind
  is wholly cloaked
    in her purple blanket
    she stands
Wrapped enough
  all will dull
    with time
Numb held me
  until I felt her full
    complete
before leaving
If she stayed,
  I'd never leave her
Numb sets me down
  we've moved
I hardly noticed
Numb sets me down
  in a place of safety
And then a whisper

Numb leaves

I never see her face

  I wonder

    if I'll ever see it

Or.

  Does seeing her face

    mean the end?

No.

  No.

I'm not ready for that

  I'll stay

The universe will not let me go

  I'll stay

The universe will not let me go

  I'll stay

            I'll stay

8. GLOWING GOLDEN

Trust

  oh what a feeling

dancing at the edge

  of my vision for days

But something

  something always

    got in the way

I wasn't ready

  so she melted away

But finally

  I met her

I feel her hand

  rest upon my shoulder

I savor the feeling

  just for a moment

    touch

I reach back

closing my hand

  over hers

    my eyes still shut

Feeling Trust

  seeing why

    she differs tonight

She has been

  so elusive

    we want to be sure

      of each other

Finally,

  I turn

And she

  is

    beautiful

Golds

  glorious patchwork

    yellows

    sunshines

dandelions

brightness

light

Blinding to anyone

but me

I see her clearly

Smile

so

so

wide

My heart

flutters

in my chest

Her fingers dance

cup my cheek

Trust speaks

a melodic voice

A voice

a little like mine

when song runs through me
You know why
  it is tonight?
I laugh

I nod
  Yes
Trust smiles
  Why?
Because,
  before
    I trusted others
Tonight
  I trust
    myself
Trust smiles
  kisses my forehead
My darling girl
  just right
The other days

I danced close,

   you trusted your friends

I nod

 So many nights

  I trusted my friends

   but I never trusted

    myself

You had me

 Trust says gently

But not all of me

 And that difference

  matters

Her hand traces my heart

You have to

 trust

  in you, darling

Tonight,

 you did

I do

I do trust myself

My journey so far

  has proved it

    time and again

Trust

  golden

  glorious

  golden

  Goddess

She lives in my soul

  never forgotten

always close

And I

  am learning that

9. TWIRLING ENDLESS MASTERPIECE

Burst of light

  free and giddy

    full

What an entrance

  Happiness makes

I drink her in

  my jaw dropped

    until I smile

      laugh

I feel so good

Happiness smiles back

  and, oh, butterflies

    in that smile

I see myself

In her eyes

I see myself

Not totally me

  no

    but

      Happiness is all I love most of myself

Her smile

  bright

    full

      bold

Her eyes

  brown

    endless

      curious

Dusted with glitter

  oh, I love a little sparkle

Happiness

  fills me

    I bubble

She wears a skirt

perfect for dancing

for endless twirls

Simple

and

black

I look down

to see I wear the same

We twirl

together

Laughter rising

feet bare

on soft moss

We wear

purple, blue

swirled

cropped tops

with cleavage

unashamed

beautiful

Happiness is

beautiful

I could end

and call her Goddess

you'd believe it all

but

Happiness?

Has wings

Wings

Fairy wings

Beautiful

gorgeous

fairy wings

Beautiful, golden yellow

with a brown center

Sunflower wings

with dandelion puffs

scattered about

Happiness is a work of art
  covered in gorgeous ink
Symbols
  words
    meanings
Of my happiness
  a riot of color
An artist's masterpiece
  my masterpiece

Happiness smiles
  It has been awhile

I nod
  I don't remember you
    quite like this
I whisper

smiling softly

I've changed
  but then
    you've changed, too

Happiness steps close
  touching my cheek
    skin like sunshine
I beam
  her baby sunbeam

You are happy for you
  I've always been here
I see your heart
  safe
  growing
  learning
You know how to be

happy for us
Not the world
    not your family
        not your friends
You,
    are happy
        for yourself

We only have this
    one chance
        this one life

I nod
    I smile
I want to live it happy
    Happy for me
Happiness beams
    Oh how you've grown
I will

always

　always

　　be here

I am your true Happiness

　And no one can steal that

I grin,

　I nod,

　　I ask her

　　　to dance with me

Happiness grins

　wings flutter

She touches my head

　　　　my heart

And I have wings, too

　for this moment

I take her sunshine hand

　and we twirl

　　we spin

we laugh

we dance

Happy for me
  I'm learning
I am my own
  glorious masterpiece
I am the main character
  in this life I live

I get one life
  I choose to live it happy
I choose happiness

10. SILVER SAFE GALAXY

I walk on

  my brain fogged

Who did I last...

  visit?

I come to

  a pool

    sit

  my feet

    at the edge

Exhaustion

  fills me

I wonder –

Before I finish my thought

  A hand on my back

A body

  behind mine

    wrapping me

      in the tightest hug

I look down

  at her arms

    covered in shimmering silver cloak

You

  I whisper

Why?

  Why has it taken

    so long to find you?

I can hear the smile

  in her deep

      deep

deep

voice

Why she smiles,

I am not yet sure

Your soul is weary

child

your body

too

even your mind

It is hard to compete with

Yes

I whisper

It is

Her arms tighten

You have not found me

but I have been with you

You didn't need to meet me

to know I was there

To know

feel

use

the protection

I offered

still offer

I nod

This is true

I've always felt her near

That smile

the deep voice

Would you like

to see me, child?

I stroke the silver fabric

realize her hands

are blackest night

And I wonder if

maybe

she isn't a being at all

If Tiredness

Exhaustion

is night personified

I wonder,

too,

if all I've met

all I will meet

are a little more goddess

a little more magic

than I first believed

Because

surely

Tiredness

Exhaustion

holds Goddess power

I smile

No

I whisper

I want to remember us

like this

with you

holding me

Is your whole cloak silver

That smile

That voice

  my body

    ripples

It is

  From the hood

    down to the floor

That surprises me.

  I hadn't imagined a hood

Will you tell me

  what your face is like?

Tiredness laughs

  I love the sound

Tell me, child

  what your heart sees

    even though your eyes are turned

A galaxy face

  Star eyes

    Star mouth

I don't hesitate

  Her face glows in my mind

You know me

  even if you don't see me

    you know me

You are so close

  to your safety

Soon,

  only pieces of you

    will be tired

She smooths my hair

I wanted to meet you

but you haven't needed me

    just yet

You, child

  just need to claim

    your rest

I nod

Claim my rest

  I've...

    I've not been so good at that

      have I?

Tiredness laughs

  We all have trouble from time to time

Sleep

  little starling

    you've earned it

Sleep,

   my little starling

I do.

ɪɪ. **RESIGNED LAMENT**

Jolted

  from Tiredness' place

    to another

      emotions spiking

They settle

Disappointment comes

  her hair dark

    past her shoulders

Taller than I am

  with a long face

I see sadness there

  mixed with

    resignation

Jolted

  again

as I realize

It was hope

  hope for better

    but she should have known

    I should have known

    that it wouldn't be

Disappointment wears blue

  blue pants

  blue top

    a darker shade

    with long sleeves

Trying to hide

  herself away

    hands curled up

    in the too-long sleeves

I look at her

  sadness, resignation

Disappointment

I tried

She nods

I know

This is not

their first offense

either

She comes over

cups my cheek

It should be near the last

Truly?

I surprise myself

with the admission

She tilts her head

Finding the true answer

for me

It won't be so frequent

You have new tools

Instead of preparing

  for an inevitable no

    preparing for disappointment

  you will have good things

Things

  and people

  who will not

  disappoint you

I nod

  nod again

  Her face

    is so

      so

        sad

  a lump forms

  in my throat

How often

   I've been

     disappointed

  in them

  since I've been little

Learning not to ask

  because I know what

   the answer is

  two letters

   to break my child heart

Disappointment

  doesn't give me a smile

I don't even think

  her face can

   move to smile

Instead,

  with soft, gentle hand

a Goddess touch

she brushes back my hair

You will make it through this too

I swallow a lump

I will?

She nods

I will come and go,

but I won't rock your world

I take a deep breath

Will your sadness ease?

Disappointment's eyes soften

Will yours?

I open my mouth

but I don't speak

I take another deep breath

and I repeat her words

I will make it through this

I will make it through anything

I will make it through everything

12. SUNFLOWER DANDELION WISHES

Laughter

  Laughter

That's how Hope comes to me

The bright

  joyous

    freeing

      laughter

        as I leave my darkness

          b

           e

          h

         i

        n

      d

Laughter bubbles

  Hope bubbles

    and I see the most

      beautiful Goddess Emotion yet

Her skin

  a plethora of rainbows

Her long braid

  a rainbow too

Hope stands naked

  proud of her body

    proud of the skin she inhabits

Along with that

  she has a broad smile

    a smile like the sun

Hope holds a bouquet

  out to me

    a cluster of sunflowers

so, so many

sunny

sunshine

sunflowers

But in her other hand

she holds a precious gift

the best gift

Hope hands me

a dandelion puff

a dandelion wish

Wish

my sweet child

Because wishes?

Wishes are hope

a very powerful hope

And you have so much hope in you

I smile

  take the wish

Thank you

  Thank you so, so much

You've not filled me

  in such a long time

I feel bubbly

     light

       free

         with wings upon my back

Hope smiles

  Oh, but darling

    you DO have wings

     you always have

I smile

  Thank her again

I feel inspired

  I feel hope

    I feel beautiful

I can love my body

  like you do

Hope smiles

  goddess, what a smile

She hands me the sunflowers

Remember darling

  Hope is only a wish away

She kisses my cheek,

  disappears,

    but I know she is with me still

Wish

Wish

Wish

13. THE SOFTNESS OF ROCK

I sit in darkness

knowing today

I won't see much

So different

from Hope

I'm not sure who I wait for

A heaviness

presses down, down on me

impossible to move

I know who it is now

Emptiness

my pulse spikes

I feel small

Yes?

I'm tired, too

    though I know she won't be here

Only a deep groan

  meets my soft query

Terror shoots

  everywhere in my body

    I can't handle her

    Emptiness

    I can't

      I screw my eyes

      shut tight

Maybe I'm a coward for it

  But why does it matter

    when I can't see anyway?

With my eyes shut

  darkness swirls

    an outline of a figure appears

though I see nothing else

A silhouette

nothing else

a lighter shade of nothing

behind my lids

I don't want you

my voice

laced with fright

trying to be strong

That groan again

I panic in my bones

You have ignored me

far too long

I shiver

body aching

with the heaviness

pressing down still

I never thought

  empty

    could mean heavy

It is too much

You demand too much of me

A groan

  If you allowed,

  I could leave sooner

I can't

I can't be empty that long

  My voice catches, again

    Damn my fear

I wonder if Emptiness even cares

Then you will continue

  to struggle

There is a hand

  behind my lids

it moves

I flinch

I feel a rough hand

made of stone

upon my cheek

Why do you fear me?

I shake my head

cheek scraping against stone

I'm too weak to survive empty

Too weak to be numb, too

I can't

I can't handle it

Emptiness sighs

like two rocks

scraping together

I am not meant like that

No?

I ask,

incredulous

  My tears flow

    absorbing into the

      rock against my cheek

In my way,

  I am meant to protect

I laugh then

  You expect me

    to believe that?

Emptiness groans

  This time,

    I do not flinch

She speaks

  A month ago?

    I would not have, no

Now?

That, child,

   is why you are here

Because you

  are finally

   able to

believe it

I shake my head

  still disbelieving

Emptiness cups

  my other cheek

   holding me captive

I allow myself

  to open my eyes

Yes?

I am greeted

   by soft, oh so soft

   eyes

set in a stone face

   long mossy tresses

It doesn't make sense

   this version of Emptiness

Safe

   you are safe

I protect

   because I allow your body

     the change to pull through

To process

   to still let you function

    Mind

     and

      body

   working separately

    leaving you

     feeling empty

Why are you stone?

  I ask,

    touching her Goddess cheek

Emptiness smiles

  I do not grow

    I am always the same

      or smaller

    worn down

      by the work you do

She moves some of the moss

  letting me hold it

And this?

  This is your growth

I shake my head

  Emptiness is so hard

    to believe

It can't be

I feel...

    I can't grow while you're around

But.

    I sense she is right

She smiles again

    I am sorry I am so strong today

        But you needed to see me

    Know me

I nod

    Yes

I shake my head

    cup her cheeks

        as she holds mine

I am glad you didn't come sooner

The heaviness leaves

    Until next time

Emptiness calls

her rough voice slowly

slowly

slowly

fading away

14. STORM GREEN BRUISES

I walk along

  as my next Emotion

    walks toward me

Jealousy

  I wasn't sure

    if she'd be a companion or not

When we meet

  I'm surprised

    to see her green

  but not the way

I'd have thought

Her green

  is bruises

    as though every moment

      I feel her

adds another hue to her skin

I see

in the sadness of her eyes

she wishes

it weren't this way

I notice, too

that even her eyes

are an ethereal green

it surprises me

that green

Jealousy

isn't shy

when she looks at me

we both know why we're here

I'm more akin

to Loneliness

she whispers

and I have to wonder

when I'll meet her

I choke on a laugh

   really a sob

I know that it is

   And that is why

      she is covered in green

         from bruises

      and not like

      the world tends to picture

Jealousy to be

I process the reasons

   Jealousy has come

So

   if I'm not lonely,

      will you go away?

Jealousy smiles

Her lips are genuinely green

   an electric lime

      as if she said fuck it

         and leaned into the color

You tell me, love

  Will I?

I sigh

  No

   I don't think so

Jealousy nods

  You've got work to do

I nod

  I'm crying now

Jealousy cups my cheek

  Her nails are nicely manicured

    green again

a good color

You'll need to do the work

I know I do

  it's Jealousy

    it's on me

Jealousy nods

  and I swear to the Goddesses

    a bruise clears

You'll get there

  the blows will be lighter

    as you settle

I nod

  what she says makes sense

You've got this, kid

  As if she's been around

    centuries longer than I have

As a Goddess,

  I guess she has

You'll get there,

  she repeats

I take a deep breath

  I nod

    Thank you

But Jealousy

  is already gone.

15. HOME, HOPE IN FRIZZY BROWN CURLS

Frustration comes

  god I know her well

Her hair?

  Frizzy

Not from humidity

  but that's another beast

No,

  it's from stress

    frizz from stress

    is simply the best

  said no girl ever

She has a crazy

  wild

    untamed

halo around her head

Frustration attempts

to tame it

knowing how easily the frizz

shows her emotions

read her

like an open book

I see her

dip her hands in a pool

wetting the frizz down

despite the effort

still

still

still

there is frizz

frizz

frizz

As if the frizz

  is causing her frustration

    and taming it

      impossible

    like poor Sisyphus

Hi

  I step closer

    feeling bold

She turns

  huffs

    as if she wasn't expecting me

You were

  supposed

    to choose anger

she retorts

I laugh

  Yeah

Yeah

I thought

I'd be there too

Frustration sighs

Well.

You're here

I nod

I am

My hair always bothers me

when it frizzes like that

I offer a smile

But.

Sometimes, it helps, too

I can visibly see

I've had a rough day

even when

I don't want to admit it

The frizz is like my acne

  stress made clear

    though far more manageable

I shrug

  I know where I am

Frustration nods

  I am more than frizz

I nod

I finally look at the rest of her

Frustration

  blue of face

    her cheeks,

    her lips

She wears

  mundane clothing

    for an Emotion

Slacks

flats

  plain blouse

She isn't adorned

  with jewels or tattoos

    and her clothing is modern

  her clothes most

like mine

No flowing togas

  no gorgeous dresses

    no nudity

The next thing I process

  are the black lines on her arm

I look at her,

  questioning

She shrugs

  All the times

    I've been frustrated

she says simply

Does...

is it only on your arm?

I am stunned

Frustration nods

For now

it only marks the incredibly rough ones

not minor ones

She meets my eyes

rich, warm

like the pages of an old book

This past year,

Frustration pauses

I'm here for a reason

I whisper softly

I chose you, Frustration

for a reason

She smiles

  the first I've seen

It was never really anger

  It was usually me

    laced with so much pain

  We did all we could

Frustration holds out her arm

  so I can see better

I gave up

  The first few weeks

    I recorded every moment

Each

  and

    every

      one

And then.

A sigh

as though it pains her to tell the story

I gave up

   I stopped recording

     each moment

I marked days

   because there was too much

I marked days

   I could breathe,

     you could, too

I made the dashes longer

   when they were days

Longer ticks

   for whole days

     of pain and frustration

I knew that

   when we met,

     I couldn't be covered

And I had to keep you going

    so one long tick

I cover her arm,

    squeeze gently

Thank you.

    For being honest with me,

        thank you.

We did our best

    Frustration breathes

You DID

    I'm still here,

        aren't I?

My grin is massive

    because I do still live

Alive for another day

    of frizzy hair

        and minor frustrations

instead of big ones

Frustration

actually laughs then

You're right

We did.

We all did

She kisses my forehead, a Goddess mark

You'll be alright

I nod

I'm learning that

I wrap my arms

tight around her

Thank you

for the reminder

Oh?

she asks,

as she hugs back

I giggle

  Yep

Of my *chaos* hair

Frustration laughs

To chaos and living

  little light

You're growing so much.

16. **FROZEN MOUNTAIN BRIDGE**

I never

ever

thought I'd be here

Dislike,

sure

But

this

this feeling

I thought she would be fire

Red.

Mixed with anger

She's hardly that

Hate

is

cold

Like a dormant mountain

no lava

no fire

A forgotten Goddess

sleeping unto revenge

Her emotion

cold

stewing

soft

unnoticed

I bite my lip

I'm not sure

what I'm meant to do

Hate

is

small

I'm glad she is

  but I see fire

    smoldering in her eyes

    it frightens me

I don't want

  to be this emotion

I know that I am

Her skin

  frosted rock

Her hair

  frozen icicles

Only her eyes hold fire

Are you going to ignore me too?

  she sneers

I flich

I know why she says it

The person I hate most

  in this world

Never

  ever

    listens to a word I say

Always misunderstanding

  never hearing

    genuinely

    truly

      what I have to say

Like frustration,

  yes

    but so much more

Tears prick my eyes

  Hate's icicles melt

Hate nods

Yeah

   It's always like that

They always melt

   You always cry

Doesn't make much sense

   Does it?

I swear

   to every goddess

Hate would drag on a cigarette,

   if she had one in hand

What

   the fuck

    do you have

to teach me?

I feel

such a wide range

of emotions

But most of all

Hate

Hate

for a woman

who was supposed

to love me always

Hate

for a woman

who now tries to

bury me

suppress me

shape me

how she believes I should be

Hate

  for a woman

    who stopped listening

      because I've nothing to say

      she wants to hear

Hate

  for a woman

    who thinks I'm not good enough

      because I don't

      fit her mold

Hate

  for a woman

    who thinks I need to be

      f   i   x   e   d

As if I can be

  f   i   x   e   d

As if

I want

  to be

    f   i   x   e   d

And I hate

  that I always cry

When Hate bubbles up,

  tears are always nearby

Hate nods

  That's how it goes

She tilts her head

  icicles still melting

You weren't really meant

  to hate

I scoff

I'm not sure

  what to do

    with that

Hate shrugs

It is true

  whether you believe it or not

Why do you think I'm cold?

  Only fire behind my eyes?

Why do you think I'm small?

  Dormant?

You were meant

  for more than me

And, honestly?

   That ain't a bad thing

How

   do I let you go

      then?

Hate laughs

Not so easy

   I'm here now

You're stuck with me

   Unfortunate as that is

I'll come

   I'll go

It may ease

  but

She shrugs

  I wrap my arms

    around my middle

But?

  I prompt

You burned that bridge

  You needed to

Until she rebuilds it

  I'll still be here

I blink

Does that mean

you're made

out of bridge?

Of wood?

Hate shrugs

One way to look at it

I nod

I sigh

I think I get it

But

You won't grow?

Unless I burn more bridges.

Hate nods

Shrugs

Like a bad knee

   twinging when weather comes

I nod

  Oh

   Okay

I think I can manage that

Her icicles

  have stopped

   melting

I've

  stopped

   crying

Hate smiles

It sucks

I know

You're nearing the end, though

  You've got brighter things ahead

Hate

  disappears

Like morning mist

Such a strange

  movement

    for a mountain

      in icicles

17. BUBBLES SPEAK TRUTH

I'm back

  surprised and stunned

    not expecting an emotion here

Confidence

  made of sparkles and bubbles

She's been buried so long

  I never expected her

Light as a feather

  but oh so

    solidly before me

She is always moving

  laughing, too

    She's laughing

I can't help myself

  I smile back

my own breast

filled

with sparkles and bubbles

Confidence takes my hand

my clothes change

I am sparkles

or at least

my dress is

Confidence spins

spins

spins

me in a dance

her laughter

the music we dance to

I think we start to float

But I'm too entranced to notice

We spin

spin

spin

until I'm

breathless

happy

elated

We float back down

Confidence looks at me

Her lips parting

in the biggest smile

I've ever seen

I've missed you, darling

I flush

but the confidence bubbling in me

tells me I needn't look away

I smile at her

You miss the girl

who sang a song about confidence

to her friend

to help her pass a test?

Confidence nods

I missed her.

yes

You miss the girl

who boldly chose to study abroad

to take classes

she knew her parents

would disprove of?

Confidence nods again

I missed her

yes

She smiles

You miss the girl

who dove head first

into a master's degree

because something would work

one way or another?

I think I've missed her most

I smile at Confidence

You've missed

the woman

who has grown so much

but has been hiding

behind her girl?

Confidence cups my cheek

That, my darling,

is precisely it

I take a deep breath

smile

You'll stay?

Confidence holds her arms out

a glorious Goddess

I never left, darling

You've always

  brimmed with confidence

You do still

  I am always with you

Tears trail

  down my cheeks

Still I don't look away

I am filled

  filled to the brim

    with Confidence

Confidence smiles

  You just have to find me

    It's alright

One by one

  her bubbles pop

her sparkles blow away

Each one

dances along my skin

then disappear

I close my eyes

letting Confidence fill me

Because that's just it

She isn't leaving

She's going back where she belongs

filling me to the brim

Riding along in my chest

18. SMOKE'S SECRET LESSON

I know who I'll find

  I've been feeling her

    for too long

But only now am I seeing her

Loneliness

  she's mostly made

    of paper bills

And credit cards

Her heart

  is a cell phone

    the beat

a text tone

Her fingertips

   are flames

      tiny little tea lights

Candles trying for hope

Her hair

   is made of scarves

      her neck

surrounded with necklaces

Her arms

   filled

      with colorful bracelets

up to her elbow

She has

a sheet mask on

and each toe

painted a different color

She turns

back made of paper

pages and pages

Books, not money

I bite my lip

I know why

she's made of these

I'm not ready for this

What

are you here to teach me?

I've learned by now

That's why they come

Loneliness looks at me
    but when she speaks
        it is only in song lyrics
if just for a moment.

She corrects
    clears her throat
        speaks
What do you think I teach you?

I want to scream
    try to take
        a breath
It doesn't come easy

You

    You're made of

       all I use

to keep you at bay

But I have no idea

    what that is meant

       to teach me

I sit on the ground

Cross my arms

    and my legs

       nearly pouting

Loneliness smiles

I try not to startle

    It, her smile,

looks weird

Until a wind tears through

Out of nowhere

a soft grey smoke

dances before me

Movements smooth, calm

A soft blue light

over her heart

and her eyes

a pale green smoke

I blink

Talk about

a Goddess transformation

What?

She comes over

  sits in front of me

    takes my hands

with her not-so-smoke ones

The lesson?

  It's okay

    Okay?

I ask

I am being

  stubborn

    I don't want

to admit this lesson

Loneliness

squeezes my hands

It's okay to feel me

It's okay to sit with me

You're safe again

You can feel lonely

without drowning

Yet you're still covering me

Cover me

hide me with bandages

and trinkets

and attempts

It's

okay

to be

lonely

I screw my eyes shut

I really

really

didn't want this lesson

I wasn't supposed

to be lonely

any longer

My voice is small

Loneliness smiles

Perhaps not

But it's okay

You're allowed to feel me

I look up

   at her smoke green eyes

      down to her smoke blue heart

Will I lose myself?

She kisses

   my knuckles

      my forehead

Have you lost yourself yet?

No,

   I whisper

      Loneliness smiles

Exactly.

I take a

deep

  deep

breath

I look at

  Loneliness

    I...

I will try

That's all I ask

  Loneliness shifts

    her heart

a phone again

Pieces, warrior

  You can use me

    pieces of me

at one time

But remember

  you're allowed

    You're allowed

to feel me

I nod

  I open my tense body

    a little stiff

but I manage

Loneliness becomes

  smoke

    truly

not solid

She settles

  in my limbs

    And we sit together

As long as it takes

It's

  okay

    to be

lonely

19. **PINK ROSE FOR LITTLE LIGHT**

My next meeting

  is as surprising

    as my last

She comes to me

  a rosy

    rosy pink

Her hair

  f

    a

    l

    l

     s

    in soft ringlets

a soft, sandy brown

Her eyes

  dance

    with mirth

      contentment

  a beautiful blue

She wears a strand of pearls

  white

  grey

  pink

Her dress

  shimmering silver

    iridescent in the light

She has

  a fancy hat

    making her ensemble

      complete

I look closer at her dress

details of mountains

in green

at the hem

Soft

green

rolling

hills and mountains

Belonging

She doesn't walk

she floats

she dances

closer to me

I smile

feeling shy

run down, too

from this journey

Meeting my other emotions

I'm left raw

especially before her.

Belonging

She takes my hand

her soft pink

spreading to me

Coating my nails

turning my clothes

to a rosy pink dress

I've got bracelets on

darker shades of pink

I feel earrings

necklace too

I suspect

   they match her pearls

Belonging

Hi

   I whisper

It feels as though

   introductions are in order

Belonging

grins

   cups my cheek

You've come so far,

   little light

We are all

very proud

I flush

You are?

For some reason

I didn't think they

talked to each other

Belonging

nods

You've found yourself

again

Beyond that

you've found home

found friends

You've found a place

where your soul

can be happy and grow

You've found me.

Was I trying

  to find you all along?

I'm puzzled

  by the idea

    but it seems good

Belonging

smiles

  The goal

    was to find yourself

You have

You've found

  a lot of yourself

    in talking to us

You still have

  more

    to learn

    to see

But you've come

  so far

    since this journey began

You feel like you belong

  yes?

I nod

  Yes, of course

    I had so much-

Belonging

shakes her head

You

  feel

    like

      you

Belong

I stare

  realization rushing through me

Yes

  I whisper

    astounded

Belonging

smiles

  That's why

    I'm here now

That's why you've found me

I think

  tears trail

    down my cheeks

I didn't realize

  in that moment

    I first felt you

      it meant?

Belonging

smiles

You've done a lot

  of hard

    and good work

      little light

Truly,

you have

You felt me there

with new friends

But it means

so much more

That's the lesson

I'm here for

That's what

I'm meant

to show you

She hugs me tight

You belong

You belong here.

In this world.

You.

Belong.

I know I'm crying now

  I squeeze Belonging

    as tight

      as I possibly can

I belong

I whisper

  knowing how much it means

    knowing how much

      I've gone through

        on this journey

I have

  much

left to heal

But

I belong

I can

take up space

space

that allows me

TO belong

to heal

I belong

She holds me tight

You always have,

little light

You just forgot

Belonging

hands me

  a rose

Pink

  pink, like her

Remember

  you belong

She turns

  to water

    the water

      settling on the petals

I belong

20. ADVENTURE

I've learned

so very much

from my Goddess Emotions

Sadness

taught me

there is safety in tears

Worry, Fear, Scared

taught me

to feel my vulnerability

Love

taught me

I need to love myself

Ache

taught me

to ache is to live

Guilt

    taught me

        that I shouldn't let her win

Numb

    taught me

        the universe will not let me go

Trust

    taught me

        she lives in my soul

Happiness

    taught me

        that I am a beautiful masterpiece

Tired

    taught me

        I need to claim my rest

Disappointment

    taught me

I will make it through this

Hope

taught me

that I am made of wishes

Emptiness

taught me

to sit in heaviness, to process

Jealousy

taught me

I've got healing to do

Frustration

taught me

to live in my chaos

Confidence

taught me

she is always with me

Hate

taught me

   some bridges need burning

Loneliness

  taught me

   that I won't lose myself

Belonging

  taught me

   I belong to this world

I reflect

  on all I've learned

   on this journey

Though,

  not every moment

   has been so easy

At times,

  emotions swirl,

   pounding at my skull

Numb fights

  to keep me so

Loneliness bangs on the door

  trying to make me believe

  I'm truly alone

And Frustration calls

  because I can't get

  myself to peace.

All the while

  Tired pulls me close

  begging me to sleep

And I beg

  for the Emptiness

  as I struggle

  not to drown

Moments like these

  I long to scream

like Ache did

Moments like these

I cry endlessly

into Sadness' pool

Moments like these

I Fear

I'm breaking

But

clarity always comes

Of all the lessons

I've seen in my soul

my heart

that I

am

capable

I can survive

any storm

This world

longs to have me

and I won't leave

As the realization

fills my soul

Someone new comes

magic sparking

from her fingertips.

She's a fairy

her body green

blossoming

Her head is a

yellow dandelion

I blink,

and suddenly

I see a dandelion puff

One more blink,

and there is an empty head

before the dandelion grows

anew

I stand

in awe

and then smile

Awe?

I ask

She fills me

with a surge of

light

power

And then

then

I see her wings

Phoenix wings

rising from her back

red

yellow

orange

Powerful

Strong

Awe smiles

You know

You've been

awe-inspiring

this whole time?

You just haven't seen it

I shake my head

but my journey

has taught me

to believe my emotions

what they have to say

Awe smiles

You're a goddess

    just as much as the rest of us

Her fingers spark with magic

    Every day

        a reason to be filled

            with awe

Around her,

    the other Goddess Emotions

        appear

Sadness

    holding Ache

        both holding in tears

Fear, Worry, Scared

    together

        Sisters three

Disappointment has her arm

    around Frustration

who holds Jealousy's hand

Love, looking less charred

comes to stand beside Awe

Happiness, glittering

stands between

Hate and Guilt

beaming, all three

Trust comes close

pride shining in her features

Tired

Emptiness

Numb

form a trio

and it make sense

how they blend

Hope and Confidence

stand together

a heady mixture

And last

Loneliness stands

beside Belonging

opposite feelings

each meaningful

I try to see them all

but I'm overwhelmed

To see so, so much

Goddess power

in one space

This journey

has opened my soul again

To see them

a rainbow of color

all I've learned

Awe steps forward

This journey

little light

starling

darling

child

love

has ended

But new

adventure

awaits

I grin

I'm full of bubbles

Yes

I suppose there is

More of you,

mixes of you

Strength

as I embrace my story

They all cheer

at my words

Awe smiles

Yes

And we all wish

to give you a gift.

Me?

But.

You're all a gift

Awe laughs

Hope speaks

Perhaps, but

you deserve a reminder

Tiredness nods

Indeed, little starling

you've earned it

I nod

  knowing each would affirm it

    if I let them

I accept

  I say

    voice strong

What is my Goddess given gift?

Awe steps close

  touching my forearm

A phoenix feather

    red

      orange

      yellow

A dandelion cluster

    green

    blue

    purple

blossoms on my arm

Between them

    Goddess of Wishes

      settles

A reminder,

  all my Goddesses chant

For always

I can't help my laugh

  I look at each of them

Thank you

  thank you all

    for this journey

I hold my arm out

  To new adventure

To living

  my story

    adventurously

www.ingramcontent.com/pod-product-compliance
Lightning Source LLC
LaVergne TN
LVHW011010200726
843509LV00011B/1044